"He has made everything beautiful in its
time."

=Ecclesiastes 3:11

For every heart searching for God's peace and the quiet wisdom of His Word.

"Deep calls to deep in the roar of your waterfalls; all your waves and breakers have swept over me."

_Psalm 42:7

I pray that every reader will experience His power through these words and through the beauty of nature.

What does God mean to me? How do I experience His love, patience, and power?

"The earth is the Lord's, and everything in it, the world, and all who live in it."
— Psalm 24:1

I find God's presence in the quiet moments, when the world slows and my heart becomes still. I meet Him through creation, reflection, and His Word, where His patient love holds me and gently leads me forward. His power is revealed not only in strength, but in grace and the quiet peace that carries me through every season.

What does God mean to you?
and how do you experience His love and presence?

"Jesus answered, 'It is written: Man shall not live on bread alone, but on every word that comes from the mouth of God.'"

— Matthew 4:4

I exalt Him, knowing that every breath I take is a gift. I see His beauty and grace woven throughout creation, and I am reminded of how fragile and vulnerable I am as a human. Yet, when I return to His Word, I find the strength my heart needs.

How has God's Word strengthened your heart during a difficult or uncertain season?

"Worship the Lord your God, and his blessing will be on your food and water. I will take away sickness from among you."
— Exodus 23:25

God is the living water of my life. Through His blessings, He grants me wisdom and sustains me, teaching me to walk faithfully through each day with trust and humility.

Have you spoken to God today? You can always count on Him, because He remains faithful and still.

"For no word from God will ever fail."

— Luke 1:37

God is faithful. Even when we feel unsure or weary, we can place our trust in Him, knowing He walks with us and makes a way, one step at a time.

Do you trust God? Can you remember a moment when, in the midst of uncertainty, you felt His presence drawing near and quietly guiding your steps?

"Trust in the Lord with all your heart and lean not on your own understanding; in all your ways submit to him, and he will make your paths straight."

— Proverbs 3:5–6

Before I knew Jesus, every step I took was wrapped in uncertainty. I didn't know if it would lead me forward or lead me astray. But now that I know Jesus Christ, I rest my trust in Him without doubt, because He walks before me and makes my path straight.

What has changed in your heart since you began trusting Jesus?

"I am a rose of Sharon, a lily of the valleys."
— Song of Songs 2:1

The Song of Songs in the Bible is one of the most beautiful books in Scripture. It is not only about romantic love, but also about God's love and how He sees you. You are the rose and the lily—you are precious to God.

How do you truly see yourself when all the noise fades away? And how much love are you willing to receive from God?

"Be joyful in hope, patient in affliction, faithful in prayer."

— Romans 12:12

Every morning when I wake up, just before breakfast, I pray to God in gratitude for how good He is and how abundantly He provides in my life. I thank Him for the blue sky, the blooming flowers, and the food on my table, no matter what the day brings.

How often do you pray? What do you usually pray about?
He is not a distant God; He is always near you.

"Set your minds on things above, not on earthly things."

— Colossians 3:2

Earthly life is not eternal; only what comes from heaven is God's promise and lasts forever. How deeply do you want to grow and dive into your spiritual life? Only what is precious from heaven and rooted in your soul can never be taken away from you.

Have you ever meditated on this verse?
Try to imagine what life will be like when you are with Jesus.

"So neither the one who plants nor the one who waters is anything,

but only God, who makes things grow."

— 1 Corinthians 3:7

God has placed a seed inside every one of us. He sees you and provid everything you need for life, helping you grow both spiritually and physically.

Have you ever tried to build something, and under God's grace, watched it grow beautifully?

"Do not be anxious about anything, but in every situation, by prayer and petition, with thanksgiving, present your requests to God."

-Philippians 4:6

I lift my prayers to God before I begin my work, sharing with Him all my challenges, especially the weight of my fears, my anger, and my anxiety. God is not a remote deity; He is present with us and attentively listening.

God knew you from the womb, and He will continue to watch over you; pray to Him instead of worrying.

"From the rising of the sun to the place where it sets, the name of the Lord is to be praised."

-Psalm 113:3

Praise is not a fleeting thanks, but a constant response, flowing from sunrise to sunset. So too is our God's love: unending and alwaysunconditional.

Praising Him constantly, from day until night.
What is something that you will always be grateful for?

"I will surely bless you and make your descendants as numerous as the stars in the sky and as the sand on the seashore."

-Genesis 22:17

Have you ever tried walking along the beach, searching for a beautiful shell? You soon find that they are plentiful—there is always one more to discover. God's blessings are far greater than we can imagine; they are so much better than anything we could ever think of.

Do you wake up with excitement, eager to witness the blessings God has in store for you today?

"For the earth will be filled with the knowledge of the glory of the Lord as the waters cover the sea."

-Habakkuk 2:14

Human knowledge is limited, but the wisdom of God is as deep and vast as the ocean. We find our way into these depths through His Word.

How often do you dive into the Bible, and how do you connect its ancient truths to your daily life?

"He makes grass grow for the cattle, and plants for people to cultivate bringing forth food from the earth."

-Psalm 104:14

Our God is both the Creator and our Heavenly Father. He created every creature with a purpose, and He will feed you just as the whole earth is His cultivated ground.

Have you ever been truly surprised by how these wild animals manage to live and thrive? It is our God who does such an amazing job of providing for them.

"God made two great lights—the greater light to govern the day and the lesser light to govern the night. He also made the stars."

-Genesis 1:16

How considerate our God is! He made the light for the day and the light for the night. Just as it was in the beginning of the world, there is the Word and there is the Light.

Have you ever gazed at a breathtaking view and wondered how such beauty exists? It exists simply because of our Lord.

"Blessed are those who hunger and thirst for righteousness, for they will be filled."
-Matthew 5:6

Hunger and thirst represent our deepest human desires. Imagine if the righteousness you crave were filled by God Himself—it would be something much deeper than just being satisfied.

What kind of righteousness are you looking for? And how would you live your life differently because of it?

"The Lord makes firm the steps of the one who delights in him; though he may stumble, he will not fall, for the Lord upholds him with his hand."

-Psalm 37:23-24

Our lives are full of challenges, and with every step we take, we may stumble. But our Lord gives us strength, and He will never leave us alone.

Have you ever been scared to climb up a long staircase? But after the climb, it always leads you to a new view.

"What no eye has seen, what no ear has heard, and what no human mind has conceived—the things God has prepared for those who love him."

-1 Corinthians 2:9

I used to be the kind of person who believed that 'seeing is believing. But I've learned there is so much more you need to see with your spiritual eyes. It feels more like a deep intuition or a feeling, and it is a beautiful gift from our Heavenly Father.

Love, hope, and faith are things you cannot see, yet you know they exist because you can feel them in your heart. So, how do you feel God's presence? What does it feel like?

"But when he, the Spirit of truth, comes, he will guide you into all the truth. He will not speak on his own; he will speak only what he hears, and he will tell you what is yet to come."

-John 16:13

Imagine wandering through a wild forest, when suddenly a holy, secret voice speaks in your head and begins guiding you through. That is the spiritual—the gut instinct and intuition in your body that I call the Holy Spirit.

Earthly life is a series of interruptions. When did you last find the solitude to listen to your heart—to that truth rising from its deepest bottom? The Holy Spirit isn't just a mystery or a distant superpowerHe dwells within you.

"You will go out in joy and be led forth in peace; the mountains and hills will burst into song before you."

—Isaiah 55:12

The sound of the wind blowing and the leaves swaying creates a melody of its own. As sunlight sparkles over the mountaintop, you realize that nature's beauty isn't just something to be seen—it is a rhythm to be heard.

As God sings through the beauty of nature, our hearts overflow with joy and praise for our Lord—the greatest and most high Majesty.

"Jesus answered, 'I am the way and the truth and the life. No one comes to the Father except through me."

-John 14:6

As a bridge between humanity and the Father, Jesus is the road leading us to truth and life. If you are struggling to find your purpose, remember that He is our Teacher and Shepherd. When you stumble, return to His Word; He is the way, the truth, and the life.

What is it like when you know the truth and the path? You can walk fearlessly, feeling that everything is secure.

"Therefore we do not lose heart. Though outwardly we are wasting away, yet inwardly we are being renewed day by day."

-2 Corinthians 4:16

Nothing is wasted. Even a cocoon needs time to transform into a beautiful butterfly. Sometimes you cannot see the change from the outside because the breakthrough must happen from the inside.

Do you know how God looks upon you? He looks at the heart, for while man looks at the outward appearance, God sees the soul. He is always with you and will never leave your side.

"These have come so that the proven genuineness of your faith of greater worth than gold, which perishes even though refined by fire may result in praise, glory and honor when Jesus Christ is revealed."

-1 Peter 1:7

God is a Goldsmith, he refines our hearts to bring out pure gold. Through our daily trials, we grow stronger and witness His grace and mercy in action.

How do you see yourself when life doesn't meet your expectations?
Do not worry, because this is the time we grow our strength through God.

"In peace I will lie down and sleep, for you alone, Lord, make me dwell in safety."

-Psalm 4:8

I find peace in my heart and feel secure because the Lord blesses my life. No matter how the day went, we should all have a good rest during the night.

In the day, we labor for our purpose; at night, we rest and prepare for what's to come. Have you experienced that quiet peace and hope at bedtime, simply knowing God is with you?

"Now you are the body of Christ, and each one of you is a part of it."

-1 Corinthians 12:27

Christianity is more than just personal salvation—it is about unity and loving each other. Every person has worth and value. As members of the Body of Christ, we are called to welcome and care for one another with true hospitality.

The church is more than a sanctuary—it is made of people in whom God lives. When we offer ourselves to Christ, we become vessels for His miraculous work.

"You will seek me and find me when you seek me with all your heart.

-Jeremiah 29:13

I can always find God's presence in nature. When I seek Him there, I find peace of mind. Nature doesn't speak through words or language, but through its very presence and its deep connection to our hearts.

When did you last feel Him near? His promise stands: He will never leave you, for His presence fills every corner of the world.

"For where your treasure is, there your heart will be also.

-Matthew 6:21"

Treasure doesn't necessarily represent money, material things, or reputation. It is something from deep within the heart, like joy, happiness, and fulfillment. It is the connection you have with God and the love you share.

May God purify our sight, washing away the filters that blur our vision, so we may truly see the eternal treasures of the heart.

"The tongue has the power of life and death, and those who love it will eat its fruit."

-Proverbs 18:21

Just as rose seeds produce roses and tomato seeds produce tomatoes, our words produce a harvest. Whatever you speak into someone's life, you can predict the result from the moment you say it.

Our words carry more weight than we think. What grows in the heart whether bitterness or gratitude—will eventually be spoken. Practice mindfulness and guard your heart; seek God in prayer, and He will provide you with peace.

"Where morning dawns, where evening fades, you call forth songs of joy."

– Psalm 65:8

Any moment can be a celebration. Whether it is finishing a project, baking a cake, or finding a sense of fulfillment—each of these moments deserves our praise and appreciation.

When was the last time you felt simply happy and satisfied? Remember that feeling, because that is true happiness.

"Walk with the wise and become wise, for a companion of fools suffers harm."

-Proverbs 13:20

Carefully choosing the right path and the right people is essential, as you inevitably become like those you associate with. This is truly the wisest advice the Bible offers.

Can you look back at what you have done in the last week? How you spend your time eventually leads you toward who you will become.

"Neither do people pour new wine into old wineskins. If they do, the skins will burst; the wine will run out and the wineskins will be ruined. No, they pour new wine into new wineskins, and both are preserved."

–Matthew 9:17

This scripture holds the deepest meaning for me. It is a vivid metaphor for the soul: new wine requires new wineskins. Once our spirits are cleansed, we cannot return to our former patterns of life. To do so would mean a disconnect between our body and soul, leading us back to the point from which we began. We must live in a state of total alignment.

I invite you to pause and meditate on this scripture once more. Seek what it is truly saying to your heart. What does it mean for you to walk this path as a Christian?

"As water reflects the face, so one's life reflects the heart."

-Proverbs 27:19

A mirror shows us our physical selves, but it takes human connection and honest feedback to reveal our hearts. In those moments of solitude, self reflection becomes the mirror that helps us understand our own inner world.

When you look in the mirror, have you ever asked yourself who you truly are? Beyond titles, identities, and nationalities, we are children of God. How God sees us is what truly matters, because we were created in His own image.

"Therefore do not worry about tomorrow, for tomorrow will worry about itself. Each day has enough trouble of its own."

-Matthew 6:34

Most of the time, we are stuck in the past or the future, but every single day is unique. There will never be another day like today. So, focus on the 'now' and immerse yourself in the present. Don't let worry become the thief of your joy.

Have you found yourself stuck in a cycle of worry? Does life feel like a never-ending race? Pause for a moment and start praying; it is the most powerful way to bring yourself back to the present. Do not worry; instead, pray.

"We have this hope as an anchor for the soul, firm and secure."

— Hebrews 6:19

Imagine a boat without an anchor. What would happen to it? It would just keep wandering, unable to settle anywhere. That must feel so uncertain. But the great thing is that we have God, and He shares His words through the Bible —wisdom that has lasted for thousands of years.

Will you open your heart and let God become the anchor of your life?
An anchor full of abundant hope and blessing.

"Those who trust in the Lord are like Mount Zion, which cannot be shaken but endures forever."

-Psalm 125:1

Being a follower of Jesus Christ doesn't mean you won't face challenges in your life, or that you will never stumble again. It is really about faith, hope, and love. To get through, you need endurance built on faith, knowing you will never be alone again. God is always with you; He is the God who cannot be shaken, the Beginning and the Forever.

Trust Him with all your heart, and then you will see how He guides you in an incredible way. May God be with you. Amen.

Acknowledgement

"How beautiful is the earth! I wonder who formed these beautiful mountains and the sky." I first heard these words from a Bible study leader six years ago. At the time, I was a very new Christian, but I had always been an adventurer someone who loved spending time in the bush, sometimes thinking deeply and sometimes just existing in the silence.

I started taking photos when I got my first camera phone around the year 2000, and I fell in love with landscape photography immediately. I am a bush wanderer with a photography habit and a philosophical mind—a mind that never tires of exploring the "why" and "how" of everything in this world. And now, here is this book.

My deepest thanks go to my godfather, Anthony Bowden. As an artist and musician, he has always told me that I am "a quill in the hand of God." His encouragement has meant more than words can say. I also want to thank my many friends from the various stages of my life—childhood, school, and the workplace. You told me you found strength through my words; I kept that in my heart and promised myself that one day I would create something beautiful to share the joy that is found everywhere.

"Jesus looked at them and said, 'With man this is impossible, but with God all things are possible.'" — Matthew 19:26

I present this book to all my friends and family. Trust in your Lord; He will bless you and walk with you always.

Deep calls to deep
A Journey Through Creation, Guided by Scripture
Copyright © 2026 W.Y

Scripture quotations marked (NIV) are taken from the Holy Bible, New International Version®, NIV®. Copyright © 1973, 1978, 1984, 2011 by Biblica, Inc.™ Used by permission of Zondervan. All rights reserved worldwide. The "NIV" and "New International Version" are trademarks registered in the United States Patent and Trademark Office by Biblica, Inc.™

First Edition: January 2026
Photography and Original Text by W.Y

Deep calls to deep
A Journey Through Creation, Guided by Scripture

The Team
Writer & Photographer: W.Y
Editor: Yu-Feng Zhang
Agent: Bianca Choi
Cover Design: W.Y

Stay Connected
We would love to hear how these reflections and images have touched your heart. For inquiries, permissions, or to share your story, please reach out via the channels below.
Email: willayeau@gmail.com
Instagram: wyfrom.waverly

"The purpose of a person's heart are deep waters, but one who has insight draws them out."

-Proverbs 20:5

www.ingramcontent.com/pod-product-compliance
Lightning Source LLC
Chambersburg PA
CBHW061052090426
42740CB00003B/125